EZARA THE ELEPHANT

Jenny Schreiber

Jenny Schreiber
Star Valley, WY 83110

In Association with
Elite Online Publishing
63 East 11400 South #230
Sandy, UT 84070
EliteOnlinePublishing.com

ISBN: 978-1-956642-74-2 (Paperback)
ISBN: 978-1-956642-75-9 (Hardback)

Meet Ezara the elephant.

**Ezara is the largest
land animal in the world.**

Ezara is an African elephant
and can weigh as much
as 22,000 pounds.

Ezara has big ears that he can
flap back and forth,
to help cool him down.

Ezara is really smart and can remember things for a long time.

Ezara's memory is so great he can recognize other elephants and humans he hasn't seen in a long time.

Ezara uses his trunk to
pick up food, drink water,
and even high-five
his friends!

Ezara's trunk has more than 40,000 muscles in it.

Ezara likes to take mud baths
to help keep himself
clean and cool.

Ezara's family is called a herd and they all take care of each other.

When Ezara was a
baby elephant he weighed
about 260 pounds and was
called a calf.

Ezara can live up to 70 years,
which is much longer
than most animals
and some humans.

Ezara likes to play with the other elephants, they use their trunks to play games like tag or soccer.

Ezara communicates with his elephant family using low rumbles that can be heard from miles away.

Ezara uses his tusks
to dig for water
or break down trees.

Ezara has thick skin that
helps him stay safe
from predators.

Ezara is a herbivore which means he only eats plants.

Ezara can eat up to 300 pounds of food in just one day!

Ezara is a great swimmer and can swim long distances.

At night, Ezara uses his big ears like fans to help him stay cool while he sleeps.

Ezara and his Elephant family are important to the ecosystem because they spread seeds and help keep forests healthy.

Ezara the elephant lives in
the desert and lush forests
of Africa.
His cousins live in the
jungles and grasslands
of Asia.

The End

Find More books by Jenny Schreiber

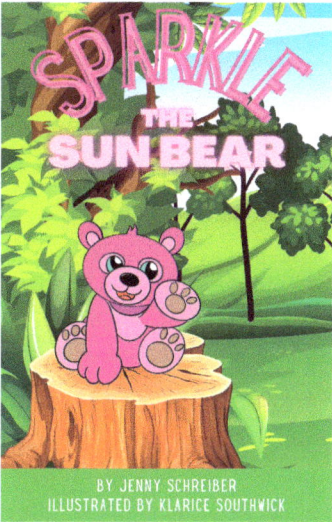

arkle the Sun Bear

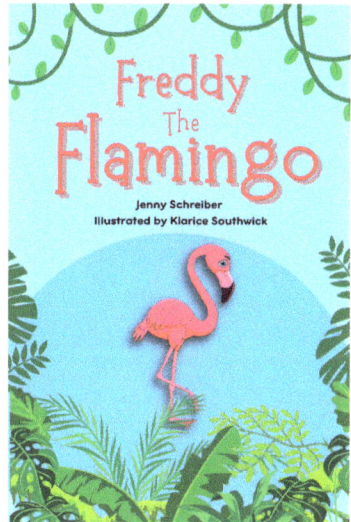

Freddy the Flamingo

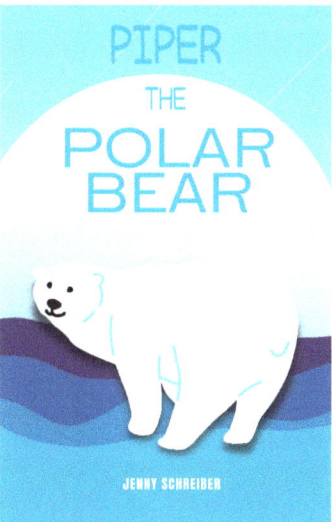

Piper the
Polar Bear

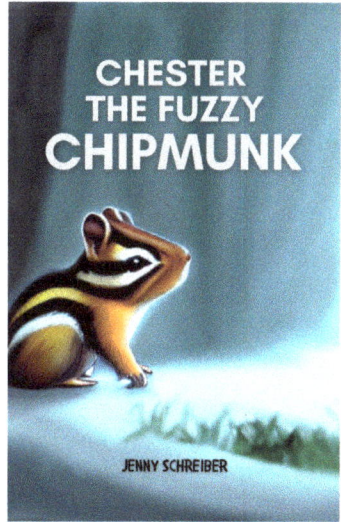

Chester the
Fuzzy Chipmunk

Animal Facts Children's Book Series

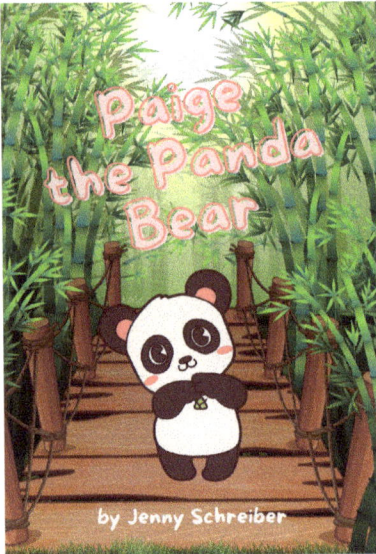

**Paige the
Panda Bear**

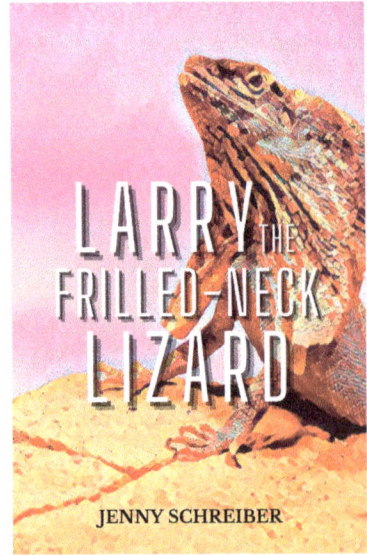

**Larry the
Frilled-Neck Lizar**

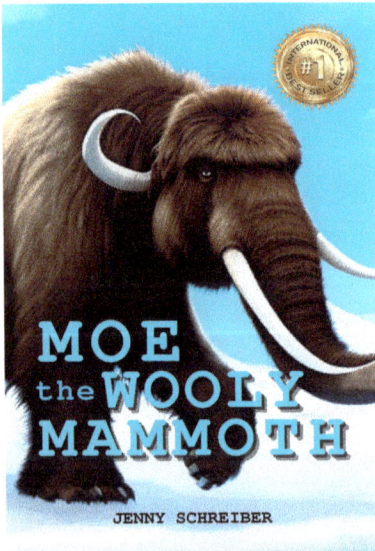

**Moe the
Wooly Mammoth**